SO-CFY-439

THE AFRICAN BURIAL GROUND

For all those who lived
For all those who were stolen
For all those who were left behind
For all those who were not forgotten

By Therese M. Shea

Gareth Stevens
PUBLISHING

Please visit our website, www.garethstevens.com. For a free color catalog of all our high-quality books, call toll free 1-800-542-2595 or fax 1-877-542-2596.

Library of Congress Cataloging-in-Publication Data

Names: Shea, Therese, author.
Title: The African Burial Ground / Therese M. Shea.
Description: New York : Gareth Stevens Publishing, 2017. | Series: Hidden
  history | Includes index.
Identifiers: LCCN 2016025669 | ISBN 9781482457872 (pbk.) | ISBN 9781482457896
(library bound) | ISBN 9781482457889 (6 pack)
Subjects: LCSH: African Burial Ground (New York, N.Y.)–Juvenile literature.
  | Slaves–New York (State)–New York–History–Juvenile literature. |
  African Americans–New York (State)–New York–History–Juvenile
  literature. | Excavations (Archaeology)–New York (State)–New
  York–Juvenile literature. | New York (N.Y.)–Antiquities–Juvenile
  literature.
Classification: LCC F128.9.N4 S54 2017 | DDC 974.7/01–dc23
LC record available at https://lccn.loc.gov/2016025669

First Edition

Published in 2017 by
Gareth Stevens Publishing
111 East 14th Street, Suite 349
New York, NY 10003

Copyright © 2017 Gareth Stevens Publishing

Designer: Katelyn E. Reynolds
Editor: Therese Shea

Photo credits: Cover, pp. 1, 27, 28 Carol M. Highsmith/Buyenlarge/Getty Images;
cover, pp. 1–32 (tear element) Shahril KHMD/Shutterstock.com; cover, pp. 1–32
(background texture) cornflower/Shutterstock.com; cover, pp. 1–32 (background
colored texture) K.NarlochLiberra/Shutterstock.com; cover, pp. 1–32 (photo texture)
DarkBird/Shutterstock.com; cover, pp. 1–32 (notebook paper) Tolga TEZCAN/
Shutterstock.com; p. 5 Keith Getter/Moment Mobile/Getty Images; p. 7 Globe Turner/
Shutterstock.com; pp. 9, 23, 25 STAN HONDA/AFP/Getty Images; p. 10 Bill O'Leary/
The Washington Post/Getty Images; p. 13 Blaue Max/Wikipedia.org; p. 14 Patrickneil/
Wikipedia.org; p. 17 (inset) Kean Collection/Getty Images; p. 17 (main) MPI/Getty
Images; pp. 19, 20 7mike5000/Wikipedia.org.

Printed in the United States of America

CPSIA compliance information: Batch #CW17GS: For further information contact Gareth Stevens, New York, New York at 1-800-542-2595.

CONTENTS

Buried History.................................4

Revealing Remains...........................6

The Real Story of New York 12

From Burial Ground to Parking Lot............18

Controversy....................................22

Laying Them to Rest 24

Memorial.......................................26

Glossary 30

For More Information......................31

Index..32

Words in the glossary appear in **bold** type the first time they are used in the text.

BURIED HISTORY

In 1991, preparation for the construction of a new federal office building in a hectic and crowded part of New York City led to a startling discovery: a skeleton. Further excavation exposed another skeleton, and another, and then another. Altogether, the bones of 420 men, women, and children were exhumed, or unearthed. Investigations revealed the bones belonged to Africans who lived during the 17th and 18th centuries. This area of New York had been a burial ground set aside for both free and enslaved Africans during colonial times.

The African Burial Ground, as it's known today, is thought by many to be one of the most important archaeological discoveries of the 20th century. It exposes much about what life was like in colonial New York for Africans, both free and enslaved.

REVEALED

The first body was found 20 feet (6 m) below the corner of Broadway and Reade Street in Lower Manhattan in New York City.

BEFORE IT'S BUILT

Before many buildings are constructed, an environmental impact study is done. Professionals study how the building would affect the people, animals, and even plant life surrounding it. Another part of the study looks into the history of the site. Historical maps indicated that the plot on which the federal building was to be built had been a burial ground. However, it was thought that previous construction projects would have "**obliterated** any remains."

This is how the African Burial Ground looks today.

REVEALING REMAINS

The bones, many in disintegrating coffins, were removed and transported to a nearby college. Then, the Cobb Laboratory in Washington, DC, was chosen to study the remains. This respected research institution is connected to historically black Howard University.

Human remains can reveal much about what a person's life was like, even how they ate. For example, scientists examined the teeth of the people found in the African Burial Ground. Faults in the teeth were evidence of poor diet. Comparing these teeth to the teeth of Africans who remained in Africa their whole life revealed that the people found in the burial ground were more likely to have suffered from **malnutrition**. Poor diets and unhealthy living conditions were likely factors.

REVEALED
The burial ground is much larger than the area that was unearthed. It's thought to cover more than 6 acres (2.4 ha).

POISONED?

Burial ground researchers found very high levels of lead in many bones. The longer the Africans had lived in New York, the higher the lead levels. Lead poisoning results in low energy, little appetite, headaches, slow body growth, hearing loss, and other health problems. It's especially harmful to children. Where did the lead come from? There's no way of knowing, but possibilities include lead in food containers or in drinks.

Manhattan

This map shows the boundaries of the African Burial Ground atop today's New York City streets.

Each exhumed skeleton was labeled with a number. Scientists recorded its condition and other identifying features. For example, "Burial 254" was the remains of a child believed to be between 3 and 6 years old. A piece of silver jewelry was found with the child, thought to be an earring or a piece of a necklace.

"Burial 205" was the skeleton of a young woman who had more fractures, or broken bones, than any of the other skeletons examined. She had shattered bones in her arms, legs, backbone, and skull, among other places. However, the scientists don't know if these resulted from a terrible accident or a violent attack.

The more we read about these and other remains, the more we think of them, not just as sets of bones, but as people with significant life stories.

BURIAL 25

"Burial 25" was a woman in her early 20s. Scientists know she died a violent death. The evidence was a **musket** ball found in her rib cage. They believe the ball was fired at her back. Her attacker either surprised her, or she was running away. Broken bones in her face reveal that she was struck. New bone growth suggests she lived a few days after the incident before dying, probably in great pain.

"Burial 259" might have been a woman dressed in a man's clothing. Possibly she was disguising herself so that she would be hired for certain kinds of work or to escape her owner.

Free and enslaved Africans in New York drove heavy carts, horses, boats, and mill equipment. An accident with one of these could crush a person to death, which could explain some of the fractures.

REVEALED

Some estimate that 20,000 more bodies may be buried in other parts of the burial ground.

At Howard University, a researcher looks at a map that details where the bodies were located in the burial ground.

Dr. Michael Blakey, an anthropologist and the scientific director of skeletal biology for the burial ground project, was one of many scientists studying the bones. He found that—shockingly—half of the Africans didn't even live to become teenagers. Others lived only a short time in the colony before they died. Undoubtedly, their hard lives had much to do with this. Their skeletons reflected a life of hardship: injured and broken bones tell of being overworked—or even worked to death.

African slaves were probably used for many different kinds of labor in the busy seaport. The role of Africans in the growth of colonial New York hasn't often been considered in the past, but the burial ground brought new attention to the issue.

ANTHROPOLOGISTS AND ARCHAEOLOGISTS

It took many kinds of scientists to unearth and examine the skeletal remains of the African Burial Ground. Anthropologists are scientists who study humans, their origins, and their ways of life, past and present. Archaeology is a kind of anthropology; archaeologists study past human life by examining bones, tools, and other **artifacts**. Many labored to carefully remove the remains so they weren't harmed in the excavation. Such work requires slow and careful effort.

THE REAL STORY OF NEW YORK

History books often focus on slavery in the American South, but African slaves were always a major presence in New York. The Dutch first established a trading post that they called New Amsterdam in 1626 on the tip of what's now Manhattan. It became part of the Dutch colony of New Netherland. The Dutch West India Company imported slaves from the Caribbean for building projects and to work in the fur trade. In 1655, the first slaves directly from Africa arrived in New Amsterdam.

There was much labor involved with building a colony. Land was cleared for houses, and docks were needed for ships. Slaves widened Native American trails and prepared them for horse-drawn carriages. Africans built and worked in sawmills to make lumber for construction projects as well.

REVEALED

There are records of a slave named Anthony the Portuguese suing a white businessman in 1638 after the man's dog hurt the slave's pig. The slave won in court.

SOME RIGHTS

Anthropologist Michael Blakey thinks slaves made up as much as 40 percent of the population of New Netherland. Under Dutch rule, slaves in New Netherland had some rights. They could marry, work for themselves when not working for their owners, and own some property. They could even sue whites. These were rights many slaves didn't have in other colonies. However, the life of a slave was still very hard. Slaves usually didn't have control over what happened to them.

"We have a standard mythology in this country of a slaveholding South and a freedom-loving North," said anthropologist Michael Blakey. The African Burial Ground reveals that's not true American history.

The first African on the island of Manhattan was a man named Jan (or Juan) Rodrigues. He was a free black sailor from Santo Domingo (now Dominican Republic) who arrived in 1613.

New York was named for James II, the Duke of York and later king of England. This picture of New Amsterdam was created the same year England took it from the Dutch.

In 1644, some slaves were allowed to farm north of New Amsterdam. They were called "half slaves" because, in return for their freedom, they agreed to share some of their grain and livestock. They also promised to work at times for the West India Company. They were later granted full freedom. This wasn't unusual for slaves under Dutch rule. There are other accounts of slaves asking for and receiving their freedom.

However, the colony of New Netherland was conquered by England in 1664 and shortly after became the British colony of New York. New Amsterdam, now New York City, grew into a busy commercial center. By 1700, the city had almost 5,000 residents. And by 1750, 20 percent of residents were Africans.

FROM HANGING TO FREEDOM

Some of the slaves who had been granted "half freedom" in 1644 had been convicted of murder a few years before! They had confessed to killing another slave. Rather than hanging them all, the court had them draw **lots** so that just one would die for the crime. The slave who was chosen was hung—but the rope broke. Rather than hanging him again, the court asked all involved to promise to continue to work and obey the law, which they did.

Life became harsher for slaves after English rule. They had fewer rights than under the Dutch. For example, no more than three Africans were allowed to meet in public. Slaves also had **curfews**. Slaves weren't even allowed to attend funerals after dark, a practice from their West African roots. These laws were a response to fears about slave **rebellions**. The British also made it harder to free slaves.

In the early 1700s, a slave market opened in Manhattan where people could buy or even rent slaves shipped from Africa, some younger than 13 years old. By the end of the 18th century, there were about 10,700 blacks in New York City and nearby Westchester County, with more than 77 percent of them slaves.

REBELLION

Slaves in New York, as in other colonies, didn't always suffer silently. Some rebelled. During an uprising in New York City in 1712, 23 slaves set fire to a building, attacked whites, and ran away. They were captured and executed. Other acts of rebellion were more peaceful, such as breaking tools needed to work or stealing a slave owner's belongings. Such acts could still be life threatening if a slave's actions were discovered.

In 1741, fires in New York City were blamed on blacks. Their accuser, an **indentured servant**, was promised her freedom for naming the wrongdoers. Many historians suspect she was lying, but some slaves were burned at the stake.

This is an image of a slave market in New York City around 1730. Slaves didn't just do hard labor. Many were skilled workers: carpenters, blacksmiths, printers, sailors, tailors, bakers, and more.

FROM BURIAL GROUND TO PARKING LOT

What happened to slaves in New York City when they died? Slaves and free blacks weren't allowed to be buried in cemeteries with whites—or even within the city. In 1673, a Dutch woman named Sara Van Borsum permitted some land she owned outside the city to become a burial ground for Africans. On maps, it was called "Negros Buriel Ground" or "Negroes Burying Ground."

We can tell that slaves had funeral services similar to colonists of the time from how they were buried. They were placed in wooden coffins with arms folded or placed at their sides. The coffin was positioned in the ground so the head was facing west, a Christian tradition. Sometimes items such as coins and beads were placed in coffins as well.

REVEALED

Only 12 slaves were allowed to gather for another slave's funeral.

WHO WAS SARA VAN BORSUM?

Historians know some facts about Sara Van Borsum. Her stepfather, a minister, was known for supporting the education of black children and for opposing wars with the natives. Sara herself was an Indian translator who received the burial ground land for helping the government communicate with Native Americans. She also received a large amount of land in New Jersey from Native Americans. She wasn't against slavery, as she owned at least six slaves.

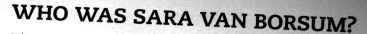

As the burial ground became crowded, coffins were buried on top of coffins. In some places, as many as four coffins were buried on top of each other.

A law to end slavery was passed in New York State in 1799. However, children of slaves were still made to work a certain number of years. All slaves in New York were finally freed July 4, 1827.

This map from the late 1700s shows the African Burial Ground at center.

By 1794, free African Americans had established the African Society, which opened a new cemetery for blacks. The African Burial Ground was closed. By that time, the city had greatly expanded. Much pressure was put on "unused" sites such as cemeteries to become land for construction. In 1795, the burial ground was divided up and sold. Since it was located in a ravine, it was covered with about 25 feet (7.6 m) of fill to level it.

Once the first buildings went up, the area's other significance became lost, especially as those buildings were torn down in preparation for new structures. By the mid-1900s, that area of Lower Manhattan was the site of many government and commercial buildings. When excavation began in 1991 for the new federal building, the site of the burial ground was just a parking lot.

MAROON COMMUNITIES

A few slaves were able to escape their masters. Escaped slaves sometimes formed settlements called Maroon communities, most notably in South America. But groups of escapees were also noted in outlying areas of New York City such as Harlem and eastern Long Island. When the city was taken over by the British during the American Revolution (1775–1783), the British promised freedom to slaves who joined their military. The city itself became a kind of Maroon community.

CONTROVERSY

There was much **controversy** surrounding the African Burial Ground after its rediscovery. Many didn't want the remains removed. They felt that exhuming the bodies and simply rebuilding over the site disrespected the memories of the Africans buried there. When Howard University took control of the excavation and research, officials promised the public that the site would be handled with reverence.

So what happened with the plans for the 34-story federal building that began the excavation in the first place? It was decided that the tower of the building—now the Foley Square Federal Office Building—would be built, but not the pavilion over the graves. Further, any new building in the entire burial ground area would require special permission. Still, many felt more needed to be done to recognize this special place.

REVEALED
The African Burial Ground was declared a National Historic Landmark in 1993.

BURYING THE PAST

How could a cemetery be hidden for 200 years? The African Burial Ground isn't the only final resting place to be covered with fill, paved, and forgotten while New York City expanded. According to the *New York Times*, about 30 of the city's parks were on land that had been church, city, or family cemeteries. In other places where construction took place, remains were either moved or left where they were, forever buried under buildings and streets.

This is a view of the African Burial Ground site in March 2006 before a special monument was built to honor it.

LAYING THEM TO REST

In 2003, the bones that had been removed from the African Burial Ground were prepared for reburial. Each skeleton was placed into a hand-carved wooden coffin made in the African country of Ghana.

Four people were chosen to symbolize the people buried in the African Burial Ground: an adult male, an adult female, a male child, and a female child. These four individuals traveled in a special procession from Washington, DC, to New York City, stopping in cities along the way where African slaves had worked. Upon their arrival on Wall Street, the four people led horse-drawn carriages carrying the coffins through the city to the site. On October 4, following an overnight **vigil**, the coffins were set into their final resting place.

REVEALED

About 10,000 people attended the Rites of Ancestral Return, a week of events marking the return of the human remains to the site after being studied for more than a decade.

GRAVE MARKERS

Because of African traditions in other places, anthropologists believe the original graves of the African Burial Ground were marked. Stone slabs have been found at the head of some graves. Still other graves were marked with wooden posts or boards connected to the head or foot of coffins. Loved ones probably held ceremonies to honor those laid to rest and continued to visit the burial ground following the ceremonies.

In 2006, the African Burial Ground was named a US National Monument, which means it's protected by the government.

MEMORIAL

In 2007, a **memorial** designed by **architect** Rodney Léon was completed. It's a tribute to the past, present, and future generations of Africans and African Americans and a reminder that they're connected. Writing on a memorial wall explains the memorial is:

> *"For all those who were lost*
> *For all those who were stolen*
> *For all those who were left behind*
> *For all those who are not forgotten."*

The ground floor of Foley Square Federal Office Building holds a visiting center for the African Burial Ground. There, people can read about Africans' role in early New York as well as the story of the burial ground, past and present. Models of the unearthed findings can also be found at the visitor center.

REVEALED

Buried with the remains are 8,000 messages written by people today to those found at the burial ground.

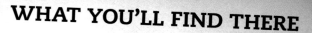

WHAT YOU'LL FIND THERE

The African Burial Ground National Monument holds a gathering space for ceremonies as well as a chamber for meditation. The Wall of Remembrance describes events involving the African Burial Ground's creation. Léon included many African symbols in the memorial as well. Visitors can follow a curving path that leads through a map of Africa, Europe, and North and South America. The center of the spiral is West Africa, where the ancestors of many African New Yorkers were from.

The African Burial Ground National Monument is a quiet place to think about the past in the noisy, crowded city of New York.

A MAYOR SPEAKS

Former New York mayor David Dinkins wrote: "Millions of Americans celebrate Ellis Island as the symbol of their communal identity in this land. Others celebrate Plymouth Rock. Until a few years ago, African-American New Yorkers had no site to call our own. There was no place which said, we were here, we contributed, we played a significant role in New York's history right from the beginning . . . Now we—their descendants—have the symbol of our heritage embodied in lower Manhattan's African Burial Ground."

REVEALED

The African Burial Ground is thought to be the only preserved 18th-century African city cemetery in the United States.

The significance of the African Burial Ground doesn't just lie in the past, but also in the present. Upon the discovery of the bones, it became important to the African American community of New York City to take ownership of the unearthing and research of the cemetery's inhabitants. These were their ancestors. In an interview with the *New York Times*, Peggy King Jorde, an official behind the burial ground's memorial, further explained, "We have been able to reach back and get a bit of the history we've lost."

With that discovery in 1991, the history of New York State should forever include the vital role of its African residents, whether slave, half-free, or liberated. Without a doubt, the city of New York rose from their labors.

TIMELINE OF THE AFRICAN BURIAL GROUND

1673 Sara Van Borsum permits land she owned outside New York City to be a burial ground for Africans.

1794 The African Burial Ground is closed.

1795 The burial ground is divided up and sold.

1991 Construction of a federal office building unearths the African Burial Ground's location.

1993 The African Burial Ground is declared a National Historic Landmark.

2003 The bones removed from the African Burial Ground are reburied.

2006 The African Burial Ground is named a US National Monument.

2007 The memorial by architect Rodney Léon is finished.

GLOSSARY

architect: a person who designs and guides a plan, project, or building

artifact: something made by humans in the past

controversy: an argument that involves many people who strongly disagree about something

curfew: an order or law that requires people to be indoors after a certain time at night

indentured servant: one who signs a contract agreeing to work for a set period of time in exchange for passage to America

lot: an object used to decide a question by its chance choice

malnutrition: the unhealthy condition that results from not eating enough food or not eating enough healthy food

memorial: something created or done to remind people of an event

musket: a type of long gun that was used by soldiers before the invention of the rifle

obliterate: to destroy something completely so that nothing is left

rebellion: an effort by many people to cause change, often by the use of protest or violence

sue: to use a legal process to get a court of law to force a person, company, or organization to give something or do something because of wrongdoing

vigil: an event or a period of time when a person or group stays in a place and quietly waits, especially at night

FOR MORE INFORMATION

BOOKS

Blashfield, Jean F. *Slavery in America*. New York, NY: Children's Press, 2012.

Cunningham, Kevin. *The New York Colony*. New York, NY: Children's Press, 2012.

Jordan, Anne Devereaux, with Virginia Schomp. *Slavery and Resistance*. New York, NY: Marshall Cavendish Benchmark, 2007.

WEBSITES

The African Burial Ground
www.gsa.gov/portal/content/101077
Read about the discovery that started it all.

African Burial Ground National Monument
www.nps.gov/afbg/index.htm
Find out more about the burial ground as well as how to tour it.

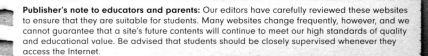

INDEX

African Society 21

Blakey, Michael 11, 13

bones 4, 6, 7, 8, 11, 24, 29

coffins 6, 18, 19, 24, 25

curfews 16

diet 6

Dutch 12, 13, 14, 15, 16, 18

Foley Square Federal Office Building 22, 26

free Africans 4, 9, 14, 18, 21

funerals 16, 18

half slaves 15

Howard University 6, 10, 22

Léon, Rodney 26, 27, 29

Manhattan 4, 12, 14, 16, 21, 28

maps 5, 7, 10, 18, 20, 27

memorial 26, 27, 29

National Historic Landmark 22, 29

New Amsterdam 12, 14, 15

New Netherland 12, 13, 15

New York City 4, 7, 15, 16, 17, 18, 21, 23, 24, 29

rights 13, 16

skeleton 4, 8, 11, 24

slave market 16, 17

slave rebellions 16

slaves 4, 9, 11, 12, 13, 15, 16, 17, 18, 19, 20, 21, 24, 29

teeth 6

US National Monument 25, 27, 29

Van Borsum, Sara 18, 19, 29